FEARLESS

CONQUERING THE FEAR THAT HOLDS YOU BACK

Published by: YM360

this book belongs to

date

FEARLESS

CONQUERING THE FEAR THAT HOLDS YOU BACK
©2016 by youthministry360. All rights reserved.

Published by YM360 in the United States of America.

ISBN 13: 9781935832607
ISBN 10: 1935832603

No part of this publication may be reproduced, stored in a retrieval system, or transmitted in any form or by any means electronic or mechanical, including photocopy, recording, or any information storage and retrieval system now known or to be invented, without prior permission in writing from the publisher.

Any reference within this piece to Internet addresses of web sites not under the administration of YM360 is not to be taken as an endorsement of these web sites by YM360; neither does YM360 vouch for their content.

Unless otherwise noted, scripture quotations are from the ESV® Bible (The Holy Bible, English Standard Version®), copyright © 2001 by Crossway, a publishing ministry of Good News Publishers. Used by permission. All rights reserved.

Author: Andy Blanks
Art Director: Laurel-Dawn Berryhill
Graphic Designer: Shane Etheredge
Copy Editor: Paige Townley

TABLE OF CONTENTS

Fearless Intro	1
Large Group Session 1 Notes	3
Small Group Session 1 Intro	5
Session 1 Getting Started	6
Session 1 Digging In	7
Session 1 Wrapping Up	9
Large Group Session 2 Notes	11
Small Group Session 2 Intro	13
Session 2 Getting Started	14
Session 2 Digging In	15
Session 2 Wrapping Up	17
Large Group Session 3 Notes	19
Small Group Session 3 Intro	21
Session 3 Getting Started	22
Session 3 Digging In	23
Session 3 Wrapping Up	25
Large Group Session 4 Notes	27
Small Group Session 4 Intro	29
Session 4 Getting Started	30
Session 4 Digging In	31
Session 4 Wrapping Up	33
Fearless Closing	34
Devotion 1	35
Devotion 2	37
Devotion 3	39
Devotion 4	41
About the Author	43

FEARLESS INTRO

WHAT ARE YOU AFRAID OF?
What are the things in your life that keep you from fully engaging in the plan God has set before you? Is it insecurity? Do you doubt yourself?

Maybe you fear how people will react to you if you stand up or stand out. Maybe you're afraid your voice doesn't matter very much. Or maybe you simply fear failure. You're living under the weight of unrealistic expectations set by you or others and you're worried what will happen if you risk making a move.

Whatever it is that you fear, you need to know this: God is calling you to face your fears.

If you're tired of your fear keeping you on the sidelines of what God wants to do through you, then FEARLESS is for you. The things in your life that keep you from having an impact on the world? They don't have to. You CAN overcome them. You can be FEARLESS. Are you ready?

HAVE YOU PREPARED FOR THE JOURNEY?
Ask yourself: Is my heart prepared to be challenged? Am I willing to be changed? If you can't answer "yes" to these questions, this journey might not be nearly as spectacular as it could be. If you need to, take a moment and silently talk to God in prayer. Ask God to radically move in your life.

YOU'RE HOLDING YOUR MAP
This book you're holding is the road map for your journey. It will help guide your experiences. Write your name and the date in the front. Hold on to it. You may want to look back and remember this time in your life.

LEARN. AND TEACH.
Keep your eyes and ears open for those valuable moments where God wants to teach you something. But don't miss the chance to teach your friends, and to be taught by them. Your friends are with you in this experience. Be open to what God is doing in and through them, and how He might be using them to speak to you. And vice versa.

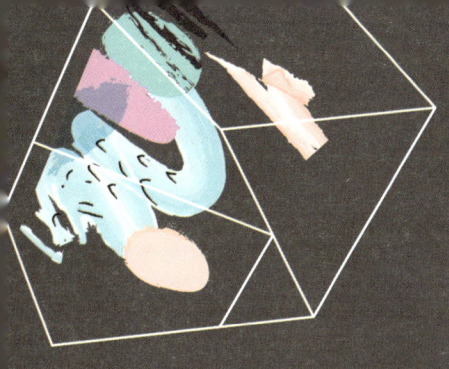

FOR GOD GAVE US A SPIRIT
NOT OF FEAR
BUT OF POWER
AND LOVE
AND SELF-CONTROL.

- 2 TIMOTHY 1:7

LARGE GROUP NOTES
SESSION 1

These two pages are designed for you to take notes on during Large Group Sessions. The stuff you're learning will really build on itself over the next few sessions. So even if you're not much of a note taker, you might want to at least jot down what you think is important.

TRY WRITING DOWN:
- Any specific teaching points
- Verse references for Scripture passages
- Quotes that make you think
- Anything you have a question about

SMALL GROUP
SESSION 1 INTRO

Much of our spiritual fear is tied to our battle with our sin nature.

We fear ourselves as much as anything.

And there's a good reason for this: Much of the time we're our own worst enemies. Can you relate to this?

But here's the deal: Jesus showed us what it looks like to be fearless in the face of temptation. He gave us a model for how to overcome our desire to rebel against God and His ways. Now, we know that Jesus, though fully God and fully man, was ultimately sinless. This is something we can never say about ourselves. But, we can say that we have the power to choose NOT to sin.

That's right. We don't have to fear sin's power over our lives. If you have come to saving faith in Christ, you've been given the power to fearlessly choose righteousness in any given situation. And while none of us gets it right every time, you should never fear that your sin somehow disqualifies you from being used by God. You should never fear that your brokenness will keep God from living and using you.

This session is all about overcoming these fears. Ready to get started?

SESSION 1
GETTING STARTED

What do you fear? Work with your group to flesh out the scale you see below.

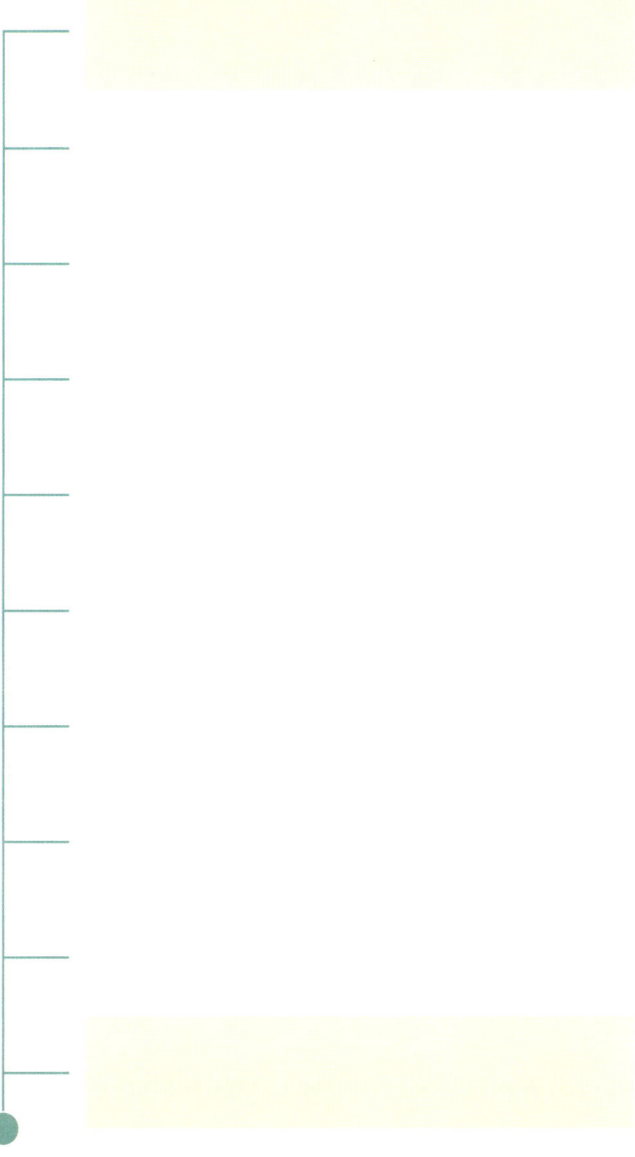

SESSION 1
DIGGING IN

Work with your group to read the passages and answer the questions below.

THINK ABOUT THIS . . .
- Do you think experiencing temptation to sin is the same as sinning?
- How aware are you of being tempted? Do you realize it when it's happening?
- Do you ever feel feelings of shame or guilt over your sin? Does it ever feel like your sin disqualifies you from being someone God could use?

PART 1: MATTHEW 4:1-4
- **Summarize what's happening in this passage.**

- **In these verses, what was Satan tempting Jesus with?**

- **What would have been the big deal if Jesus had just turned rocks into bread?**

- **How did Jesus respond to the devil and what can we learn from it?**

- **Here's a bigger question: Could Jesus have sinned?**

- **Why is it essential that Jesus lived a sinless life?**

PART 2: MATTHEW 4:5-7

- **Satan wasn't finished! What did the devil tempt Jesus with in these verses?**

- **Can you guess why this might have been tempting to Jesus?**

- **What was Jesus' response?**

PART 3: MATTHEW 4:8-11

- **What did Satan do this time? And what was Jesus' response?**

- **What can we learn from Jesus' example here?**

> "NO TEMPTATION HAS OVERTAKEN YOU THAT IS NOT COMMON TO MAN. GOD IS FAITHFUL, AND HE WILL NOT LET YOU BE TEMPTED BEYOND YOUR ABILITY, BUT WITH THE TEMPTATION HE WILL ALSO PROVIDE THE WAY OF ESCAPE, THAT YOU MAY BE ABLE TO ENDURE IT."
>
> - 1 CORINTHIANS 10:13

> "SUBMIT YOURSELVES THEREFORE TO GOD. RESIST THE DEVIL, AND HE WILL FLEE FROM YOU."
>
> - JAMES 4:7

SESSION 1
WRAPPING UP

Temptation is something I am not strong enough to overcome.

There is sin in my life. God will not use me to impact the world.

I am fearful in the face of sin and temptation.

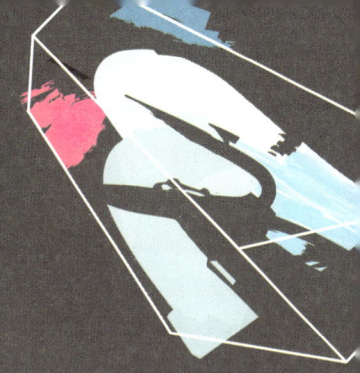

THEN JESUS SAID TO HIM, "BE GONE, SATAN! FOR IT IS WRITTEN, 'YOU SHALL WORSHIP THE LORD YOUR GOD AND HIM ONLY SHALL YOU SERVE.'" THEN THE DEVIL LEFT HIM, AND BEHOLD, ANGELS CAME AND WERE MINISTERING TO HIM.

- MATTHEW 4:10-11

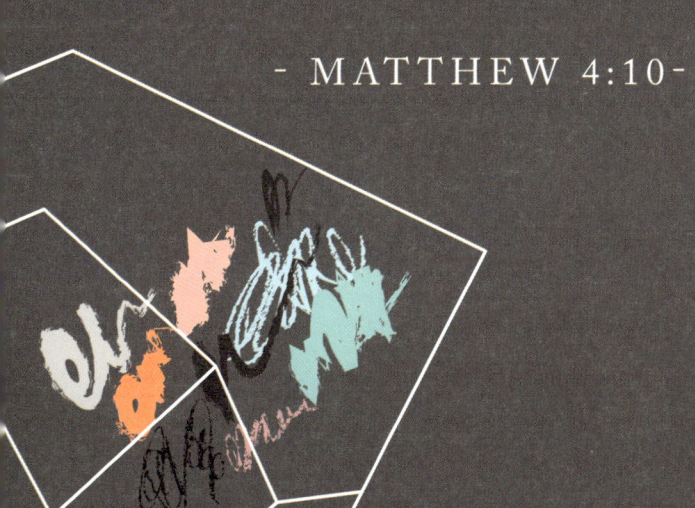

LARGE GROUP NOTES
SESSION 2

These two pages are designed for you to take notes on during Large Group Sessions. The stuff you're learning will really build on itself over the next few sessions. So even if you're not much of a note taker, you might want to at least jot down what you think is important.

TRY WRITING DOWN:
- Any specific teaching points
- Verse references for Scripture passages
- Quotes that make you think
- Anything you have a question about

SMALL GROUP
SESSION 2 INTRO

Who are you? It's an important question, isn't it?

In fact, people who study teenagers and adolescent development say that identity formation is a huge part of what it means to be a teenager. Much of your teenage years are spent figuring out who you are. Does that sound familiar to you?

If you're being transparent, you might admit that much of the fear and insecurity you feel is tied to your identity. The fear of being singled out or ridiculed is a real one. So much of this is tied to doubt about who you are. It's OK if this describes you. It's pretty common for most if not all teenagers. Want to know something cool? Jesus encountered this very thing.

You see, Jesus was put in a situation where people very much doubted His identity. What you're going to see in this session is that Jesus fearlessly stood firm on His identity, proving that He was who He claimed to be. We can do the same thing.

As you seek to navigate the world you live in, there should never be any doubt about the nature of your identity. If you are a Christ-follower, your identity is hidden in Jesus. Paul says your old life is gone. In its place is a life lived for Christ.

SESSION 2
GETTING STARTED

What is their true identity? Work to see who can be first to correctly guess the real identities of the famous individuals below.

KATY PERRY	BATMAN	BRUNO MARS	JAMIE FOXX	CATWOMAN

DRAKE	SUPERMAN	CAPTAIN AMERICA	VIN DIESEL	WOLVERINE

WORD BANK

KATHRYN HUDSON

AUBREY GRAHAM

ERIN MARLON BISHOP

MARK SINCLAIR VINCENT

PETER GENE HERNANDEZ

BRUCE WAYNE

STEVE ROGERS

CLARK KENT

JAMES LOGAN HOWLETT

SELINA KYLE

SESSION 2
DIGGING IN

Work with your group to process through this time of Bible study.

Spend some time talking through the following questions with your group.

Come up with a few situations where it's hard for teenagers to be themselves. (If you choose, use the space below to write your answers.)

Come up with a quick list of emotions a person might feel who finds himself or herself in these situations.

In the situations you've discussed, what would be some reasons teenagers might be tempted to hide their true identities?

Is there anything wrong with changing who you are to fit the situation? Explain.

[1] And when he returned to Capernaum after some days, it was reported that he was at home. [2] And many were gathered together, so that there was no more room, not even at the door. And he was preaching the word to them. [3] And they came, bringing to him a paralytic carried by four men. [4] And when they could not get near him because of the crowd, they removed the roof above him, and when they had made an opening, they let down the bed on which the paralytic lay. [5] And when Jesus saw their faith, he said to the paralytic, "Son, your sins are forgiven." [6] Now some of the scribes were sitting there, questioning in their hearts, [7] "Why does this man speak like that? He is blaspheming! Who can forgive sins but God alone?" [8] And immediately Jesus, perceiving in his spirit that they thus questioned within themselves, said to them, "Why do you question these things in your hearts? [9] Which is easier, to say to the paralytic, 'Your sins are forgiven,' or to say, 'Rise, take up your bed and walk'? [10] But that you may know that the Son of Man has authority on earth to forgive sins"—he said to the paralytic—[11] "I say to you, rise, pick up your bed, and go home." [12] And he rose and immediately picked up his bed and went out before them all, so that they were all amazed and glorified God, saying, "We never saw anything like this!"   - Mark 2:1-12

Read the passage with your group and answer the questions below. If you want, use the space provided after each question to write your responses.

- **Read verses 1-4. Summarize exactly what's going on here by describing the scene surrounding the story.**

- **What do the crowd's actions, including the actions of the four men, say about who they believed Jesus to be?**

- **Look at verses 5-7. What is surprising about Jesus' response?**

- **What is the issue the scribes have with Jesus? What is their problem?**

- **Now look at verses 8-11. Jesus responded to the critical thoughts of the scribes. What can we learn from His response?**

- **Explain why Jesus replied the way He did. What was He accomplishing?**

- **In verse 12, the man walks. What did this prove?**

SESSION 2
WRAPPING UP

Work with your group to have a discussion all about what your identity is built on.

I have been crucified with Christ. It is no longer I who live, but Christ who lives in me. And the life I now live in the flesh I live by faith in the Son of God, who loved me and gave himself for me.
- Galatians 2:20

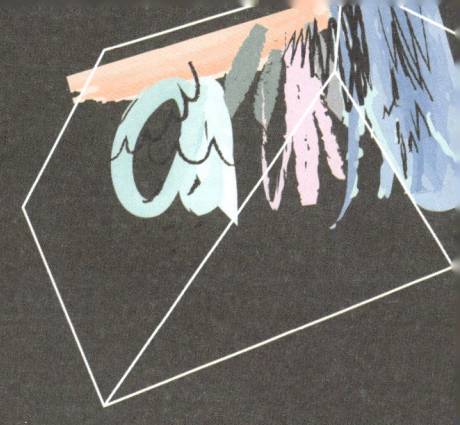

"BUT THAT YOU MAY KNOW THAT THE SON OF MAN HAS AUTHORITY ON EARTH TO FORGIVE SINS"—HE SAID TO THE PARALYTIC—'I SAY TO YOU, RISE, PICK UP YOUR BED, AND GO HOME.'"

- MARK 2:10-11

LARGE GROUP NOTES
SESSION 3

These two pages are designed for you to take notes during Large Group Sessions. The stuff you're learning in this session is building on the stuff you learned in the first two. So, even if you're not much of a note taker, try to write down what you think is important.

TRY WRITING DOWN:
- Any specific teaching points
- Verse references for Scripture passages
- Quotes that make you think
- Anything you have a question about

SMALL GROUP
SESSION 3 INTRO

Sometimes it's hard to take a stand. It's OK to admit it. Sometimes it seems like you're the only person who is trying to stay true to what you believe. But just because it's difficult doesn't mean you shouldn't take a stand. After all, Jesus went through this very thing.

When it feels like you're the only one doing the hard thing because it's what God has called you to do, it can be easy to want to find another way out. Jesus did. Hours before His crucifixion, Jesus asked God if there was a different way. A way that wasn't so difficult. And yet, even in His asking, Jesus was fearless. "Let this cup pass from me; nevertheless, not as I will, but as you will."

As you seek to live as Christ-followers, you are called to model Jesus' boldness. Yes, the road is hard sometimes. But being a part of God's mission to redeem the world makes it worth it. The right thing is often the hardest thing to do.

In this session, you'll be challenged to embrace the tough times by imitating Jesus' fearlessness. Are you ready?

SESSION 3
GETTING STARTED

Doing awesome stuff is something hard.
Read these three stories with your group.

STORY 1:

The youngest person to climb Mt. Everest, the tallest peak in the world, is a 13-year-old American boy named Jordan Romero. Jordan became the youngest climber to reach the top of Mount Everest by surpassing the previous record set by a 16-year-old Nepalese. Jordan risked death and injury by summiting. Dozens of people die each year on Everest, while hundreds of others get sick or suffer other injuries. When he summited, he did what any teenager would do. He called his mom. "There were lots of tears and 'I love you! I love you!'" his mother said. "I just told him to get his butt back home."

Source: http://www.cbsnews.com/news/13-year-old-reaches-top-of-mt-everest/

STORY 2:

When Jedh Barker was a 20-year-old Lance Corporal serving in Vietnam, he did something that would earn him the Congressional Medal of Honor, our nation's highest military award. During a patrol, a large enemy force attacked Barker's squad, causing numerous casualties. Although wounded, Barker boldly remained in the open, firing his machine gun with devastating results. Realizing that Barker was a threat, the enemy directed their fire on his position. He was again wounded, preventing him from operating his vitally needed machine gun. Suddenly, an enemy grenade landed in the midst of the few surviving Marines. With complete disregard for his personal safety, Barker threw himself upon the grenade, absorbing with his body the full force of the explosion. In a final act of bravery, he crawled to the side of a wounded friend and administered first aid before succumbing to his wounds. He gallantly gave his life for his country.

Source: http://www.cmohs.org/recipient-detail/3223/barker-jedh-colby.php

STORY 3:

Ashley Fiolek is someone for whom breaking stereotypes comes naturally. Ashley routinely beats the competition in motocross, a typically male dominated sport. And if that wasn't enough of a challenge, Ashley was also born deaf. Despite the inherent dangers of motocross, and the difficulties caused by her disability, Ashley goes after it 100%. Racing since she was 7-years-old, she has won a host of awards including the Women's Pro National Motocross Championship and an X-Games Super-X Gold Medal.

Source: https://en.wikipedia.org/wiki/Ashley_Fiolek

SESSION 3
DIGGING IN

Work with your group to process through this time of Bible study.

FIRST, READ MATTHEW 26:36-39.
What are your general observations? Write down three things that stand out to you as important.

Now, answer the following questions:
- We can't know for sure, but can you imagine what must have been going through the minds of Peter, James, and John when they saw Jesus become "sorrowful and troubled"? What do you think they might have been feeling?
- Why would it be so unusual for them to see Jesus this way?
- Just so we're all on the same page, what was Jesus so distressed about?
- Why did Jesus want the "cup" to be taken from Him?
- Ultimately, how did Jesus deal with the fear, sadness, and anxiety He was struggling with?

NEXT, READ MATTHEW 26:40-42.
Again, write down two or three things that you think are meaningful.

Now, answer these questions:
- The disciples are contrasted with Jesus here. We know Jesus' mindset. How would you describe the mindset of the disciples?
- Why was Jesus' message to Peter so fitting? What would Peter soon find himself in the midst of?
- Jesus went back and prayed the same prayer a second time. What does this tell you about how He was dealing with what was about to happen to Him?
- The prayers are slightly different from verse 39 to verse 42. What do you see different in verse 42? What does it say about Jesus' mindset?

NEXT, READ MATTHEW 26:43-46.

One more time: write down two or three things that stood out to you in this passage.

Next, answer these questions:
- The moment that all of creation had been holding its breath for was about to happen. Jesus was about to go to the cross. What were the disciples doing again?
- What does this say about God's view of His mission and humankind's view of His mission?
- Verse 44 says something amazing. If Jesus already knew God's answer, what was the purpose of His prayers?
- So here's something to think about: When Jesus woke up the disciples, it was too late. They had slept through their chance to be with Jesus in the moment He needed them most. They failed to see God's mission at work right in front of them. What did it cost them?

"[7]But we have this treasure in jars of clay, to show that the surpassing power belongs to God and not to us. [8]We are afflicted in every way, but not crushed; perplexed, but not driven to despair; [9]persecuted, but not forsaken; struck down, but not destroyed; [10]always carrying in the body the death of Jesus, so that the life of Jesus may also be manifested in our bodies. [11]For we who live are always being given over to death for Jesus' sake, so that the life of Jesus also may be manifested in our mortal flesh. [12]So death is at work in us, but life in you."
- 2 Corinthians 4:7-12

SESSION 3
WRAPPING UP

When do you most feel like a cardboard box, fragile and a little worthless?

Rewrite verse 7 substituting "I" for "we" and "me" for "us."

Write down a time when standing up for what you believe in left you a little confused.

Rewrite verse 8 replacing the words "We are" with "I am"

When are you most likely to feel insecure about your faith?

Rewrite verse 9 in the space below, adding the phrase "I am" at the beginning.

"⁷But we have this treasure in jars of clay, to show that the surpassing power belongs to God and not to us. ⁸We are afflicted in every way, but not crushed; perplexed, but not driven to despair; ⁹persecuted, but not forsaken; struck down, but not destroyed; ¹⁰always carrying in the body the death of Jesus, so that the life of Jesus may also be manifested in our bodies. ¹¹For we who live are always being given over to death for Jesus' sake, so that the life of Jesus also may be manifested in our mortal flesh. ¹²So death is at work in us, but life in you."
- 2 Corinthians 4:7-12

AGAIN, FOR THE SECOND TIME, HE WENT AWAY AND PRAYED, "MY FATHER, IF THIS CANNOT PASS UNLESS I DRINK IT, YOUR WILL BE DONE."

– MATTHEW 26:42

LARGE GROUP NOTES
SESSION 4

You know what to do with these two pages by now, right? Use them to take notes during your Large Group sessions. By now you've figured it out: this stuff matters! This could be a time in your life you look back on as pretty important. So, write down anything that stands out to you as something you might want to hold on to.

TRY WRITING DOWN:
- Any specific teaching points
- Verse references for Scripture passages
- Quotes that make you think
- Anything you have a question about

SMALL GROUP
SESSION 4 INTRO

Let's face it, it's tough to be a teenager. Sure, grown-ups sometimes give you a hard time for all the drama you seem to always find yourself in the middle of (sure, sure . . . it's not your fault . . . ever). But here's the deal: even adults remember what it was like to be a teenager. And if they were honest, even they'd admit it isn't easy.

You live in a world where people come at you from every angle, criticizing, ridiculing, and abusing trust. It can be overwhelming to navigate the relational waters of your worlds. But you can take heart! These struggles are not a surprise to God.

See, Jesus experienced great opposition. And He knew His followers would too. He reminds and encourages us to remember that He is with us, and that in the end, He and His people will be victorious. There is no room for fear because the end has already been written. And you win.

As you wrap up your study of Fearless, this lesson will help give you confidence to face anything that others throw at you, all through your trust in God.

Let's finish strong. Ready? Turn the page and let's get started.

SESSION 4
GETTING STARTED

HOMEWORK IS _____

BECAUSE _____.

INSTAGRAM IS _____

BECAUSE _____.

SPORTS ARE _____

BECAUSE _____.

MY SCIENCE TEACHER IS _____

BECAUSE _____.

BOYS ARE _____

BECAUSE _____.

GIRLS ARE _____

BECAUSE _____.

I AM _____

BECAUSE _____.

SESSION 4
DIGGING IN

Work with your group to process through this time of Bible study.

Let's get real for a moment. Why is it so hard to be made fun of or singled out because of your faith? Why does it make us want to shrink?

Why do we let other people's words or actions impact us so much?

What do we have to lose by allowing people to silence us or to minimize our influence?

What is the alternative way for us to respond?

Read the following passage and answer the questions below:

"I tell you, my friends, do not fear those who kill the body, and after that have nothing more that they can do. But I will warn you whom to fear: fear him who, after he has killed, has authority to cast into hell. Yes, I tell you, fear him! Are not five sparrows sold for two pennies? And not one of them is forgotten before God. Why, even the hairs of your head are all numbered. Fear not; you are of more value than many sparrows." - Luke 12:4-7

- Right out of the gate, Jesus is addressing what we have been talking about. Summarize what Jesus says in verse 4-5.

- Jesus isn't saying we should "fear" Him in the sense of the word as we might understand it. Jesus doesn't want us to fear Him. So, what do you think He might be saying?

- What do verses 4-5 say about our priorities in life?

- Jesus mentions birds in verses 6-7. What is He saying here?

- How does this work to reframe, and maybe even soften Jesus' tone in verses 4-5?

"I have said these things to you, that in me you may have peace. In the world you will have tribulation. But take heart; I have overcome the world." - John 16:33

- What does Jesus offer that is the opposite of tribulation and trouble?

- In the midst of all the craziness and tough times that we face, how can Jesus offer peace? What does this look like?

- What does it mean that Jesus has "overcome the world"?

- How does this help us navigate the stress and the mess that we find ourselves dealing with?

- Bigger question: how can this truth keep us from being fearful? How does it help us lead BOLD faith-lives?

SESSION 4
WRAPPING UP

ONE QUESTION:
WHAT IF WE LIVED OUR LIVES WITH ONE SINGULAR MOTIVATION: THAT WE WOULD HONOR GOD IN EVERYTHING THAT WE DID?

How would this impact your friendships?

How would this change the way you engaged with people at school?

What would this do to your family reactions?

How would this impact your relationship with God?

FEARLESS CLOSING

Being fearless for you may look differently than what being fearless looks like for someone else. For some people being fearless is embracing a newfound faith. For others, it's a sense of hope they've not had in a while . . . or ever. For others, living fearlessly will mean they've just finally let go of the junk that's holding them back. Being fearless can mean a lot of things. But here's what it doesn't mean . . .

Living fearlessly doesn't mean becoming a spiritual superman. You're going to make mistakes. You're going to fall short. The devil wants to beat you up with your mistakes, making you feel shamed by your failures. Don't let him. Living fearlessly doesn't mean being perfect. Living fearlessly means that when you do mess up, you dust yourself off, refocus on Christ, and keep moving forward.

Over the course of the last four sessions, you've had the chance to face many of the things that make you fearful. Now that you've faced your fears, the key to living fearlessly is to trust that God is whom He says He is, and that He has done what He said He would do. It's that simple. Because if that trust is there, then all you do is live your life with your eyes fixed on Jesus who made a way for all of us to live in freedom. That freedom is fearless. One more time: the freedom that Christ offers us through the cross is FEARLESS.

This way of fearlessly living your faith? It's contagious. When you're truly changed, truly set free, you can't help but tell someone . . . and that's how the Gospel is shared. When we are fearless on the inside, we can't help but live that way on the outside.

BE BOLD. LIVE FEARLESSLY!

FEARLESS
DEVOTION 1

This is the first of four Fearless devotions. Find some time to work through them during your study of Fearless.

In Genesis 12, God tells the aging Abram (who would become Abraham), that even though he was childless, he would become the father of a great nation. This presented some interesting issues for Abram and his wife Sarai (who would become Sarah). They were way past childbearing years. Like, not even close. To believe that God would see this plan through would take great faith.

Read Genesis 18:9-14. Sarah had a moment where she doubted God's plan for her. She had already taken matters into her own hands before this, encouraging Abraham to get her maid pregnant. It was almost as if Sarah was forcing God's hand, trying to make God's promise happen according to her timetable. Sarah was proving to be someone for whom a trusting faith was difficult to come by.

But here's the cool thing: God honored Sarah's faith, shaky though it was. He was faithful in giving Abraham and Sarah a son, Isaac, thus fulfilling the promise He made to them.

God expects you to be faithful. But He allows room for our weakness.

As we consider what it means to live a bold, fearless faith, we have to know that we're going to make mistakes. We're going to blow it. God would much prefer that our faith in Him never waivered. After all, He's never done anything to justify anything less than 100% confidence from us. But, He knows that we struggle with our sin-nature. He knows we will sometimes fall short of what He commands in us. And because He loves us, He is willing to meet us where we are and pull us through.

Next time you're in a spot where you're tempted to be fearful, and your faith is wavering, trust God to fill in the gaps. And respond in boldness.

SOMETHING TO THINK ABOUT . . .

1. Can you think of a time when your faith was wavering and God gave you the strength to stay true to Him? What was the outcome?

2. Remembering how God has intervened in your life is an important aspect of your faith. Why? What's so important about recalling how God has helped you in the past?

3. Say a prayer (or write it down if you want) to God thanking Him for always being there to pick you up when you fall. Ask God to give you a spirit of boldness and a steady faith. But praise Him for being willing to take you as you are and for shepherding you to a stronger faith.

God, I am consistently falling short of your glory. But through it all I know you love me endlessly & I don't deserve it, no one does. I pray that next time I am tempted, you will become clear in my foggy, unseeing eyes! I will be reminded of your boundless love.

FEARLESS
DEVOTION 2

This is the second of four Fearless devotions. Find some time to work through them during your study of Fearless.

"I volunteer! I volunteer as tribute!" Do you remember that scene in the first Hunger Games movie? These were the words that permanently changed Katniss Everdeen's life. She volunteered to replace her younger sister in a televised death match with teens and children from across their country. Facing eminent death, Katniss traded her life to save her sister. Although deeply afraid, she faced a seemingly insurmountable scenario head on. Katniss overcame odds that were certainly not in her favor in a bloodthirsty battle arena full of peers who were determined to kill her.

As you know, Katniss ultimately survived. Furthermore, her volunteerism and acts of valor in the arena became the center of a revolution against the evil in her land. Her resolve ushered in a wave of hope.

God expects you to be faithful. But He allows room for our weakness.

Stephen was a man of great resolve who spoke with a fiery conviction about the sins in his land—sins that penetrated every element of society around him. He definitely wasn't fearful. Religious leaders didn't like his bold approach, and ultimately stoned him to death for his bold preaching. He became the first martyr, or person who died for his faith. Just before he died, he prayed for God to forgive the very people who stoned him, much like Jesus had prayed for those who crucified Him. Talk about someone who was fearless!

It takes guts to stand for what you believe in even in the face of death. Do you want the resolve of Stephen in your life? Are you ready to boldly speak the truth even if it means worldly scorn and suffering?

SOMETHING TO THINK ABOUT . . .

1. Why is it easy to shy away from conflict, especially conflict over what you believe?

2. While we don't ever want to come across as a jerk, why is it important to be bold in how we talk about our faith? Why is it important not to let fear or discomfort keep us from being true to what we believe?

3. Spend some time in prayer to God today asking Him to reveal to you places in your life where you need His help being bold. You may consider writing these down. Ask Him to help you be fearless in representing Him.

FEARLESS
DEVOTION 3

This is the third of four Fearless devotions. Find some time to work through them during your study of Fearless.

There's a state park in Georgia where you can rent kayaks and then paddle along a trail through a dense forest canopy of cypress trees growing right of the water. Sometimes the trail gets dark even on a sunny day with such thick foliage overhead. The trees all resemble one another so it's quite easy for a person to become separated from his or her group of paddlers temporarily—or even lost for a while! Thankfully someone had the foresight to nail small reflective signs onto the trees at moderate intervals to point paddlers in the right direction. Those little reflective signs offer the peace of mind. They give the assurance that a kayaker is still on the right trail. Simply follow the signs and eventually arrive back at the dock.

Take out your Bible or Bible app and check out John 1:6-9.

John was called by God to point people toward the coming arrival of Jesus on earth. He was to live his life in such a way (fearlessly!) that people could see that his passion and desire was for something more than selfishness and temporary fame. Much like the little signs nailed to the trees on the water trail, John's testimony—the bold way he lived his life—was a means for people to see through life's obstacles and dark shadows and onward to the hope that would come through the blood of Jesus.

John called Jesus the "true light." John's life mission was to reflect the true light of Christ, no matter what anyone else said about him. By living to please God, John pointed people to Jesus. Like the water trail signs guide a separated paddler back to the security of the dock. John guided people toward the eternal security found in knowing Jesus.

Where does your life point? Be challenged today to live your life in a way that points people to Jesus.

SOMETHING TO THINK ABOUT . . .

1. When we don't live boldly, when we allow our fear to keep us from living on mission for God, what does that do to the impact God wants us to have?

2. What would have happened if John worried more about what people thought about him than he did about wanting to please and honor God? What would have happened to his influence?

3. Pray to God today asking Him to remind you of how important you are to Him and His mission. God chose to create you (He didn't have to) because He wants you on mission with Him. God's desire is to work through you to lead others to Himself. Pray for a spirit of boldness in how you project your faith to the world.

FEARLESS
DEVOTION 4

This is the fourth and final Fearless devotion. Find some time to work through them during your study of Fearless.

The web is flooded with videos of veterans returning from overseas and reuniting with their dogs, commonly referred to as "man's best friend." Take a few moments to do a simple YouTube search for "Military Reunion With Man's Best Friend." Watch the videos, some of which have had millions of views. Pretty cool, right?

You'd be hard pressed to find a more faithful friend than a dog. Even after months and months of deployment, the troops' furry friends never forgot them. Some are even still waiting for owners who won't ever return home due to paying the ultimate price for freedom.

Faithfulness makes dogs never waiver from their loyalty and devotion to their owners. Faithfulness makes a soldier never waiver even if it means months away from family and the very real possibility of dying in combat. Jesus' faithfulness led Him to complete His earthly mission, defeating sin and the grave. But His faithfulness doesn't end there.

Check out how far Jesus' faithfulness really goes in John 14:1-4.

If you have a saving relationship with Christ, you're promised an eternal place in heaven with Jesus after this life ends. Jesus won't even fail you when your earthly body dies! More than anything, this should be the motivation for you living a bold faith life. The Scripture passage today ought to comfort you especially in times of doubt and danger.

Strive to be a faithful follower of Jesus first and then in every other relationship in your life second. By doing so you'll experience deeper friendships and a tighter family bond, but you'll know God better than you can imagine. You'll truly know what it lives to pursue your faith fearlessly.

SOMETHING TO THINK ABOUT . . .

1. Who is the most faithful person in your life? What is it about them that makes them so faithful?

2. How can you model the faithfulness of Christ in your relationships? What are some ways you can seek to do this?

3. In what ways does Jesus' faithfulness encourage you to be faithful in all you do? List three to five ways.

4. Don't forget to make some time to pray with God today. Thank Him for the faithfulness He has shown you. Pray that you would be bold in your faith, fearlessly showing faithfulness to God and to those people whom He has put in your life.

ABOUT THE AUTHOR

ANDY BLANKS

Andy is the Co-Founder and Publisher for YM360. Andy lives in Birmingham, AL with his wonderful wife Brendt, their three daughters, and one son. He's a pretty big fan of both the Boston Red Sox and anything involving the Auburn Tigers. When he's not hanging out with his family or volunteering at his church's youth ministry, you can find Andy trail running or mountain biking.

Fearless was inspired by the excellent book, *Facing Your Fears*, by Bethany Barr Phillips. *Facing Your Fears* is a 40-day devotional that is offered as the Follow Up Journal to this study. For more information on *Facing Your Fears*, go to: ym360.com/fears

IF YOU'RE A NEW OR A YOUNG CHRIST-FOLLOWER, THIS BOOK IS A MUST-READ.

New: First Steps is a powerful journal that will help you learn exactly what it means to have a new life in Christ. You'll learn about God, about the Gospel, and about how to take the first steps on your new journey with Christ.

"NEW" WILL TEACH YOU...

4 weeks of biblically solid, interactive, and creative daily devotions

Important articles dealing with key issues of your new faith

Charts, verses, lists, and more to help you understand the Bible

Guides to help you go deeper in your faith when you're ready

TO VIEW SAMPLES OF NEW & TO ORDER, GO TO YM360.COM/NEW

YOU HAVE AMAZING POTENTIAL TO IMPACT YOUR WORLD FOR CHRIST.

NOT TOMORROW. RIGHT NOW!

Your chance to be used by God isn't just some time in the future. It's now! Your world is rich with opportunities to share the message of the Gospel, and to show people the amazing difference Christ can make in their lives. NOW equips you to make just such a difference.

"NOW" WILL HELP YOU...
- Understand the PURPOSE God has in store for you
- Catch God's VISION for exactly how He wants to use you
- PRACTICE real, practical ways to impact your world
- Commit to ACTING on the opportunities God is giving you

TO VIEW SAMPLES OF NOW & TO ORDER, GO TO YM360.COM/NOW